Desserts
AROUND the WORLD

by Lisa M. Herrington

Children's Press®
An imprint of Scholastic Inc.

Library of Congress Cataloging-in-Publication Data
Names: Herrington, Lisa M., author.
Title: Desserts around the world/Lisa M Herrington.
Description: First edition. | New York: Children's Press, an imprint of Scholastic Inc., 2021. |
  Series: Around the world | Includes index. | Audience: Ages 5–7. | Audience: Grades K–1. |
  Summary: "This book shows young readers some of the many ways people eat dessert
  around the world"—Provided by publisher.
Identifiers: LCCN 2021000156 (print) | LCCN 2021000157 (ebook) | ISBN 9781338768763 (library binding) |
  ISBN 9781338768770 (paperback) | ISBN 9781338768787 (ebook)
Subjects: LCSH: Desserts—Juvenile literature. | Food habits—Juvenile literature.
Classification: LCC TX773 .H4476 2021 (print) | LCC TX773 (ebook) | DDC 641.86—dc23
LC record available at https://lccn.loc.gov/2021000156
LC ebook record available at https://lccn.loc.gov/2021000157

10 9 8 7 6 5 4 3 2 1   22 23 24 25 26

Printed in Heshan, China 62
First edition, 2022

Series produced by Spooky Cheetah Press
Cover and book design by Kimberly Shake

Photos ©: cover top left, 1 top left: JGI/Jamie Grill/Getty Images; cover bottom right, 1 bottom right: BSIP/Universal Images Group/Getty Images; 4 left: NourineT/Stockimo/Alamy Images; 4 center: Mandy Cheng/AFP/Getty Images; 5 left, 5 right: Stockbyte/Getty Images; 7: Belinda Howell/Getty Images; 8: Kontrec/Getty Images; 9: JGI/Jamie Grill/Getty Images; 10: Kelly Sillaste/Getty Images; 12: Ruaridh Stewart/ZUMA Press/Newscom; 13: Ernesto Arias/EFE/Newscom; 15: jeu/Getty Images; 16: lupengyu/Getty Images; 18: Peter Lourenco/Getty Images; 19: baona/Getty Images; 21: andresr/Getty Images; 22: GMVozd/Getty Images; 23: Thais Ceneviva/Getty Images; 26–27 background: Jim McMahon/Mapman®; 26 top: Image Source/Getty Images; 26 bottom: Steve Russell/Toronto Star/Getty Images; 27 top left: Catalina Zaharescu Tiensuu/Dreamstime; 27 top right: uniquely india/Getty Images; 27 bottom: Simon Reddy/Alamy Images; 28 left: Annapustynnikova/Dreamstime; 28 right: sbossert/Getty Images; 29 bottom center: chengyuzheng/Getty Images; 29 bottom right: Yauheni Labanau/Dreamstime; 31: wundervisuals/Getty Images.

All other photos © Shutterstock.

The desserts shown on pages 4 and 5 are: cannoli (Italy); snow ice (Taiwan); berry pudding (Ukraine); trifle (England); and s'mores (United States).

TABLE of CONTENTS

introduction
JUST LIKE ME

Kids in every country around the world have a lot in common. They go to school and play. They have families and friends. Still, some things—like their favorite desserts—can be very different!

ITALY

TAIWAN

UKRAINE

Trifle is an English dessert. It is made of cake, fruit, and **custard**, jelly, or cream.

ENGLAND

UNITED STATES

5

chapter 1
COOL CAKES AND COOKIES

Cakes make special events extra special! Australia is known for its lamingtons—square yellow cakes coated with chocolate and coconut. In Germany, Black Forest cake is a favorite. This chocolate cake is made with layers of whipped cream and cherries.

Germany's Black Forest cake usually has three or four layers.

In Australia, school bake sales are often called "lamington drives."

Macarons in France come in many colors and flavors.

Some people love their cookies chewy. Others like them crunchy. You get both tastes with macarons (mah-kah-ROWNZ)! These cream-filled cookies are a hit in France. Chocolate chip cookies are the most popular choice in the United States. They were invented in Massachusetts in the 1930s. Back then each cookie was the size of a quarter.

The first chocolate chip cookies were made with chopped-up chocolate bars.

chapter 2

BREAKFAST FOR DESSERT

In Vietnam, some kids eat green waffles ... for dessert! The color comes from green pandan plants. The pandan leaves are mixed with coconut milk to give the waffle **batter** a sweet taste. In Belgium, warm waffles are topped with powdered sugar for a tasty treat.

Belgian waffles came to the United States in 1962. They were first served at the World's Fair in Seattle, Washington.

In Vietnam, people usually eat pandan waffles without toppings.

People around the world love doughnuts!
In Peru, doughnuts are called picarones
(PEE-ka-rohn-es). They are made from squash
and sweet potatoes and drizzled with syrup.
Loukoumades (loo-koo-MAH-thez) are eaten
in Greece. These fried dough balls are soaked
in honey and sprinkled with cinnamon.

Loukoumades are thought to be the oldest-known dessert in the world!

Picarones are a favorite street snack in Peru.

13

chapter 3

POPULAR PIES AND PASTRIES

Pies and **pastries** often combine yummy fillings with delicious **crusts**. Banoffee pie is a favorite in England. It is made with bananas, cream, and toffee. Haupia (HOW-pee-uh) pie comes from Hawaii. It features two types of pudding: chocolate and haupia.

Haupia is a traditional coconut-flavored Hawaiian dessert.

England's banoffee pie is named after its two main ingredients: bananas and toffee.

Baklava is cut into small pieces before it is served.

You can find tasty pastries around the world. In Turkey, baklava is made of thin layers of dough filled with chopped nuts and covered in honey. Apple strudel is a sweet treat in Austria. Bet you can guess its fruit filling! The sliced apples are often mixed with raisins, sugar, bread crumbs, and walnuts.

Austria's apple strudel is cut into slices to serve.

Egg tarts are enjoyed in different parts of the world. In China, they are called dan tats. The creamy filling is made from milk, eggs, and sugar. It is poured into a flaky shell and then baked. In Portugal, egg tarts are sometimes dusted with cinnamon before serving. They are called pastéis de nata (pash-TAYS duh NAH-tah).

Portuguese egg tarts are baked in a very hot oven. The high heat creates brown spots.

China's egg tarts are crispy outside and gooey inside.

19

chapter 4

DIFFERENT TASTES

There seems to be a dessert for just about every taste! Some people love cold or creamy desserts. Gelato (JEH-lah-toe) is a frozen treat from Italy. It is like ice cream. In Japan, rice cakes called mochi (MOE-chee) are wrapped around an ice cream filling.

In Japan, mochi are believed to bring people good luck.

Gelato means "frozen" in Italian!

21

Some people go crazy for chocolate! Brazil is known for its brigadeiros (bre-GA-de-ros). These chocolate balls are covered in sprinkles. Many people in the United States like chocolate fondue. They dip fruit and other treats into melted chocolate.

Cheese fondue is popular in Switzerland. That dish gave a New York chef the idea for chocolate fondue.

Brigadeiros are eaten at many celebrations in Brazil.

Fruit brings flavor to desserts like mango sticky rice in Thailand.

Believe it or not, rice is part of many desserts around the world. Some people in Senegal like to eat sombi. This creamy **porridge** is made of cooked rice and sweet coconut milk. In Thailand, sticky rice is flavored with coconut milk and often served with mango.

The world is filled with delicious desserts, from sweet rice dishes to tasty cakes. What is your favorite?

In Senegal, sombi is eaten warm or chilled.

IF YOU LIVED HERE . . .

Let's look at some more desserts around the world!

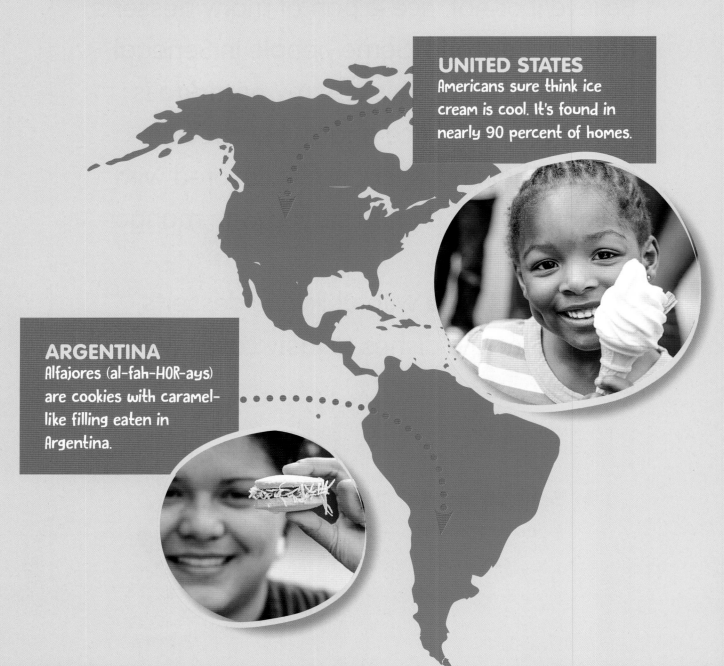

UNITED STATES
Americans sure think ice cream is cool. It's found in nearly 90 percent of homes.

ARGENTINA
Alfajores (al-fah-HOR-ays) are cookies with caramel-like filling eaten in Argentina.

FRANCE
A French favorite, crème brûlée (KREM broo-LAY) is a custard topped with a thin layer of hardened sugar.

INDIA
One of the most popular sweets is gulab jamun (goo-lahb JAH-muhn). These deep-fried doughnut balls are soaked in a sugary syrup.

EGYPT
Om Ali (Uhm AH-lee), a type of bread pudding, is the national dessert.

A CLOSER LOOK

Check out some amazing birthday desserts around the world.

Mexico

Pastel de tres leches means "three milks cake." It gets its name for a good reason! After baking, the cake is soaked in three kinds of milk.

Australia and New Zealand

Pavlova cake has a crisp crust topped with whipped cream and fruit. It is named after Russian ballerina Anna Pavlova.

Sweden

Swedish princess cake is covered with a green, candy-like topping. The cake got its name because princesses were said to like it.

Mini pavlovas are a handheld treat!

United States

American kids blow out candles on all kinds of cakes. They include ice cream cakes, character cakes, and colorful cupcakes.

China

Guests at birthday parties in China may be served these peach-shaped desserts. The pretty peach buns represent a long life.

Russia

Russian honey cake takes a while to make! That's because the dessert is often stacked with ten thin layers of cake that are separated by frosting.

GLOSSARY

batter (BA-tuhr) a mixture used to make cakes and other baked goods

crusts (KRUHSTS) the crisp outer layers of pastries or pies

custard (KUHSS-tehrd) a sweet, thick dessert made from milk, eggs, sugar, and sometimes other flavorings

egg tarts (EG TARTS) baked pastries filled with custard

ingredients (in-GREE-dee-uhnts) the items used to make something, such as the foods used in a recipe

pastries (PAY-strees) pies, tarts, and other sweet baked goods

porridge (POR-ij) a kind of hot cereal made by boiling oats or other grains in milk or water until the mixture is thick

INDEX

ABOUT THE AUTHOR

Lisa M. Herrington has written for children for 20 years. But she has loved desserts her entire life! She lives in Trumbull, Connecticut, with her husband and daughter. At Christmastime, she especially enjoys eating her family's Italian anginetti cookies frosted with a sweet citrus glaze.